WORLD DOMINION
THE HIGH AMBITION OF RECONSTRUCTIONISM

WORLD DOMINION

The High Ambition of Reconstructionism

PETER MASTERS

THE WAKEMAN TRUST * LONDON

WORLD DOMINION
THE HIGH AMBITION OF
RECONSTRUCTIONISM

© Peter Masters 1990
First published 1990 in *Sword & Trowel*
This book edition 1994

THE WAKEMAN TRUST
5 Templar Street
London SE5 9JB

ISBN 1 870855 16 7

Cover design by Andrew Sides

Printed in Great Britain by The Alden Press, Oxford

CONTENTS

1. Describing Reconstructionism

RECONSTRUCTIONISM is the name given to a movement which has arisen since the mid 1960s in the USA, and which now draws growing support throughout the West from people of reformed persuasion on the one hand, and charismatic persuasion on the other. Reconstructionists believe that Christian people have been given a mandate by God to bring the world, with all its social and political institutions, under the authority of God's law – including the entire Mosaic civil code. By this activity, as well as by the Gospel, Christians are to secure dominion over the world, and thus establish the kingdom of God on earth in readiness for the return of Christ.

Many American reconstructionists want to see the government of the USA following and enforcing all the laws of the Old Testament right down to the implementation of Old Testament economic policy. To accomplish this in the United States would, they suppose, not only save that nation from disaster, but also provide a demonstration of godly government to the world. Other nations would then speedily imitate the USA, and so the social-political dominion of the people of God over all the earth would eventually come to pass.

Reconstructionists teach that the great commission of Christ to His disciples goes beyond the work of evangelism. In their view it includes this quest for the social-political dominion of the world; the persuading of all nations to submit to the rule of Israel's ancient laws. *Dominion* is a much used term among reconstructionists, and it means exactly what it says – that Christians are to seek dominion over all human society during this present 'kingdom' age. Reconstructionist teaching is commonly called 'dominion theology'.

Another term which crops up quite often in the reconstructionist vocabulary is *theonomy*. This literally means – God's law – but it has been popularised by reconstructionists to describe their particular view of God's law, namely, that *all* Old Testament law (including the punishments for disobedience) continues to be binding on all society today.

Yet another term which peppers the books and magazines of reconstructionists is the more familiar word, *theocracy.* In their use of this word reconstructionists refer to a Christian civil government which enforces the moral, social and economic laws of the Old Testament. Such a government at present nowhere exists, but reconstructionists are sure that it will, just as soon as evangelical Christians can be persuaded that they have lost sight of God's commission to seek dominion over the social and political institutions of their nations.

Readers may by now have realised that the people most likely to adopt reconstructionist ideas are those who hold postmillennial views. Postmillennialists believe that Christ's kingdom on earth (the church) will grow so mightily in size, strength and influence that the world will become totally 'Christianised' before the return of the Lord.

Amillennialists and premillennialists expect a final apostasy at the end of the age, when 'evil men and seducers shall wax worse and worse'. This obviously stands in complete contrast to the reconstructionist vision of a world under the dominion of an all-powerful, triumphant church.

Certainly all the founders of reconstructionism are convinced postmillennialists. Charismatics who embrace reconstructionism are not so easily classified. Some are postmillennial, but many – strange as it may seem – are postmillennial-premillennial. They believe in both schemes at once, taking the view that the world will be almost entirely won for Christ, and will be under the dominion of the church, before His return. Then, at His return, Christ will usher in the millennial glory. The original Presbyterian (postmillennial) reconstructionists and the charismatic new recruits have this in common – they abominate the 'doom-millennialism' of others. They want an entirely victorious scenario for the end times: a victory both in terms of *numbers* converted, and in political supremacy also.

Many charismatics in the UK – including many of the house churches – hold to this kind of theology. They reject any picture of spiritual decline and moral depravity prevailing in the final stage of this present age, adopting instead a picture of mighty world-wide revival and restoration. Even now this restoration is underway, or so they believe. After nineteen hundred years of marking time or edging forward at a snail's pace, the kingdom of God is now back on the march, heading into a season of spectacular evangelism and social dominion. This kingdom of God is, to their view, chiefly composed of charismatic groups, and it will conquer the world for Christ, swallowing up the remnants of traditional evangelicalism as it does so.

Numerous American charismatics use the language of reconstructionism very freely. *Dominion theology* and *kingdom theology* are familiar terms. They also associate openly with Presbyterian reconstructionists. The latter (for all their staid reformed credentials) have gleefully encouraged every alliance. They have decided that they need the charismatics.

It is, incidentally, important to remember that when disaffected charismatics find their way into non-charismatic churches, they often carry with them their highly triumphalist dominion theology of the last days. Many have learned to depend on the rhapsodic celebration of restoration and dominion *now*, to bolster and sustain their faith. The non-charismatic churches to which they go will have to teach them a more biblical view of the 'last things', and also teach them to exercise true faith, without the aid of artificial stimulants.

Many charismatic groups which are not directly identified with reconstructionism approve of much of the teaching. American televangelist Pat Robertson – who attempted to run for the presidency of the USA – is an example of a leading charismatic who has very strong reconstructionist sympathies, while remaining outside the camp.

Reconstructionists, then, see it as the duty of Christians to bring about a 'restored paradise on earth' (their own term) before the coming of Christ. It will be a republic patterned on the 'ideal' framework for society given to ancient Israel before the arrival of the monarchy. The nations of the world must be persuaded, step by step, to adopt the Mosaic law-code, and to reconstruct government so that the functions of the state are strictly limited to the administration of law and order and the maintenance of national defences (until reconstructionism has advanced to the point where war is banished).

As the result of reconstruction, governments would have no welfare responsibilities. These would fall to the churches and the voluntary goodwill of the public. Democracy would be abolished as anti-biblical, and the civil power would enforce the laws of Moses using precisely the same punishments as those laid down for ancient Israel. The death sentence would apply to murder, the striking or cursing of parents, unchastity, homosexuality, rape, apostasy, idolatry, unfulfilled prophesying, disobedience of a court order, and a host of other offences. (As far as reconstructionist author Dr Greg Bahnsen is concerned, even Sabbath-breaking is to be included in the long list of offences which should be punished by death.) According to some writers, Presbyterianism would be enforced and Jewish garments would be worn, with no mixing of fibres permitted in cloth.

Before the reader loses patience and considers such ideas to be the irrelevant notions of cranks and crackpots, we must warn that this movement appears to have enormous appeal for many very able and serious people. We must therefore review its claims.

2. The Founding Authors

THE BEST-KNOWN NAME among the founders of reconstructionism is that of Dr Rousas J. Rushdoony, an American Presbyterian minister and scholar of reformed convictions, now the elder statesman of the movement. In 1965 he formed an organisation, known as the Chalcedon Foundation, to propound his ideas. (This foundation publishes *The Journal of Christian Reconstruction*.) Dr Rushdoony moved gradually to the position of advocating 'the social-political mandate' for God's people, and the continuing binding force of all Old Testament law for every nation. He published his huge work – *Institutes of Biblical Law* – in 1973. This treatise probably marks the *true* beginning of the reconstructionist movement.

In his book, *God's Plan for Victory*, Dr Rushdoony

affirms that one's view on the return of Christ is critical to reconstructionism. He speaks of America as having 40 million Christians, and wishes that all these could be converted to postmillennialism. Then, rather than merely preaching the Gospel to snatch brands from the burning, they would be among those – 'preparing to conquer the world and assert the "Crown Rights of King Jesus" '. Nothing less than global dominion for the church is in Dr Rushdoony's view. Most of his 30 books are devoted to the advocacy of some aspect of reconstructionism.

Dr Greg Bahnsen is another principal author whose name is known in the UK (probably on account of his book *Homosexuality: A Biblical View*). Having studied theology at Westminster Theological Seminary, and philosophy elsewhere, he has held appointments both as a seminary lecturer and a pastor. He greatly advanced reconstructionist ideas through a book entitled – *Theonomy in Christian Ethics*. In this 650-page intensive work, Dr Bahnsen made the novel claim that the Lord Jesus, in the sermon on the mount, said that He had come to *confirm* the law. This was Bahnsen's highly peculiar and untenable exegesis of the word translated *fulfil* in *Matthew 5.17.*[*]

By this approach Dr Bahnsen was able to teach that the Saviour commanded the Christian church in all

---

[*]See Appendix 1.

ages to uphold the *entire* Old Testament law-code (with the exception of ceremonial rites) to the letter. Every subsequent command or commission of Christ to His disciples is seen to include this basic duty of promoting throughout the world the enforcement of *all* the laws of God, including the entire Hebrew social system. The great commission of the Lord is therefore regarded as a reiteration of what reconstructionists call the *dominion mandate.* This is the command of *Genesis 1.28* – 'Be fruitful, and multiply, and replenish the earth, and subdue it: and have dominion . . .' (Reconstructionist author Gary North asks in one of his books – 'How can we disciple the earth if we are not involved in running it?') Greg Bahnsen issued another pro-reconstructionist book in 1985 under the title – *By This Standard: the Authority of God's Law Today.* This book will be referred to again later in this chapter.

The third significant name among the founding authors of reconstructionism is that of Dr Gary North, who is a PhD economist, and a former editor of Rushdoony's magazine, *The Journal of Christian Reconstruction.* Dr North has now written more than 25 books, among them Christian critiques of secular economic trends, and Christian investment advice. Others are titles which promote reconstructionism. Gary North's style is colourful, energetic and hard-hitting to the extent, at times, of exaggeration and immaturity. (These aspects of his writing style have been sharply criticised by some of his own camp in the USA.) He has issued a stream of books written by himself and others under a variety of imprints – *Spurgeon Press, Geneva Ministries, Institute for Christian Economics* and *Reconstruction Press.* All these 'publishers' are based at a little place called Tyler, in Texas, where Dr North lives and works. It is Gary North, incidentally, who enthusiastically advocates biblical stone-throwing as the divinely instituted and ideal method of execution for wrongdoers, not least on account of its cheapness.

In describing his own books, Dr North summarises his views for us. Concerning *The Dominion Covenant: Genesis,* he says: 'It is specifically an economic commentary . . . What does the Bible have to say about economic theory? Does it teach the free market, or socialism, or a mixture . . . or something completely different? *The Dominion Covenant* answers these questions by setting forth the biblical foundation of economics. It offers the basis of a total reconstruction of economic theory and practice . . . practical guidelines by which Christians are to reconstruct civilisation.'

In promoting his book *Backward, Christian Soldier? – An Action Manual for Christian Reconstruction,* Gary North writes: 'Jesus said, "Occupy till I come." But if Christians don't control the territory, they can't occupy it. They get tossed out into cultural "outer darkness", which is just exactly what the secular humanists have done to Christians in the 20th century: in education, in the arts, in entertainment, in politics . . . Today the humanists are occupying . . . If Christians adopt a vision of victory and a programme of Christian reconstruction, we will see the beginning of a new era on earth: the kingdom of God manifested in every area of life. When Christ returns, Christians will be *occupying*, not hiding in the shadows . . . This book shows where to begin.'

These three prominent founder-figures have been joined in recent years by a vigorous group of seemingly able minds and active pens. It must be said that *some* of the literary output of reconstructionists would meet with strong approval and agreement from all reformed Christians. Herein, however, lies the danger. Dr Greg Bahnsen's book, *By This Standard*, is a case in point. In a 372-page book of 31 chapters, the first 200 pages (20 chapters) are for the most part a well-argued presentation of the abiding character of Old Testament moral law. Taken as a refutation of the most 'primitive' kind of dispensationalism, and also of Calvinistic antinomianism, these pages ably present the essential arguments. Most reformed readers would strongly agree with most of this material. But then, from page 201, Dr Bahnsen sharply takes leave of orthodox evangelicalism. The foundation he lays in the first portion of the book does not even remotely support the views which he proceeds to unfold.

Dr Bahnsen picks up the 'first use' of God's law recognised by the Reformers, which was the *political* use: that is, that the civil magistrate must enforce the law of God. He affirms this, and rebukes evangelicals for ignoring this function of God's law. However, most evangelicals are quite certain that God's *moral* law is authoritative over all society, and that governments should make laws which reflect God's standards. In this belief countless Christians have protested to their governments about lax laws on such matters as abortion and homosexuality. The argument is whether the *entire* Old Testament law-code (plus penalties) is intended to be imposed by Christians on unregenerate society. Is this what the Reformers meant when they said that the first use of the law was a political use? Of course not! The idea is a gross distortion of history.

3. The Crucial Error

THE ESSENCE OF reconstructionism is stated by Dr Greg Bahnsen in these words – 'Repeatedly the New Testament authors assume the standard of the law in their ethical themes and make application of the law in their moral judgements. Every scripture, every point, every word, and indeed every letter of the Old Testament law is upheld in the New Testament. Therefore, it would seem obvious that the socio-political aspects of the Old Testament law would retain their validity today – that they are authoritative for civil magistrates of all ages and cultures.'

It should be obvious that this is an extremely careless statement, because *every* detail of the Old Testament law-code is certainly not upheld in the New Testament as an 'ongoing' standard either for the church or the world. The punishments of the Old Testament are not reiterated and prescribed anywhere in the New. In *John 8*, for example, the Lord Jesus Christ does not want the woman taken in adultery to be put to death by stoning. Likewise Paul does not advocate stoning for the Corinthian sinner *(1 Corinthians 5.3-5 and 12-13)*. In this case the guilty man is expelled from the church. This, Paul tells us, put him under the *direct* judgement of God. The church administered some of the punishment (withholding of membership and fellowship) but the Lord did the rest, for – 'them that are without God judgeth'. (It is worth noting that if reconstructionists had their way, a similar offender today would be executed in accordance with *Leviticus 20.11*, in which case he would not have the opportunity to come, over time, to repentance, and consequently the church would never be able to forgive him in obedience to *2 Corinthians 2.6-8*.)

Nowhere in either *Acts* or the epistles is there any reference whatsoever to a number of the 'sundry laws' of Moses (ie: those supplementary civil rules described in the page-titles of the *Authorised Version* as 'Divers Laws and Ordinances'). It is quite mistaken to say that 'every letter of the Old Testament law is upheld in the New Testament.'

Where, for example, is there in the New Testament any reference to the battlement law of *Deuteronomy 22.8*, or the prohibition of mixed seeds (verse 9), or the prohibition of different sorts of thread such as wool and linen being mixed (verse 11)? Where in the New Testament is the law upheld which banned illegitimate children from the congregation of the Lord even to the tenth generation *(Deuteronomy 23.2)*? Where do we find the law enforcing marriage after promiscuous sex upheld and prescribed for the ongoing nations of the world *(Exodus 22.16)*, or the law against joining public demonstrations *(Exodus 23.2)*, or that against the sale of land *(Leviticus 25.23)*?

Where do we find in the New Testament the death sentence upheld for a rebellious son, a homosexual person, or a medium *(Deuteronomy 21.18-21; Leviticus 20.13 and 27)*? The sweeping claims of reconstructionists simply cannot be substantiated. Indeed, it is made quite clear in the Old Testament that some laws applied *only* to the Jewish nation. In *Deuteronomy 23.3-4*, for example, it is expressly stated that Ammonites and Moabites were banned from the congregation – 'Because they met you not with bread and with water in the way, when ye came forth out of Egypt; and because they hired against thee Balaam . . . to curse thee.' Here it is made very clear that this rule had exclusive relevance to the Jews, and only then for a given period of about 250 years. It is simply not true, therefore, to say that every portion of law is permanently binding into the Christian age, and upheld as such in the New Testament. The reconstructionist notion of the nature of the

Mosaic law is easily demolished by many similar observations.

The orthodox evangelical understanding of the status of Old Testament law is expressed in both the Westminster and Baptist Confessions in an almost identical way. Chapter 19 (of both Confessions) begins by asserting the abiding status of the *moral* law – the *law of universal obedience* – written in the heart of Adam and his posterity. This continued as the perfect rule of righteousness after the Fall, and was later published to mankind in the ten commandments given on Mount Sinai.

The Confessions proceed to speak of the *ceremonial* laws of Israel, with their rites and duties, which were appointed only until the coming of Christ. Then the Confessions speak of the other laws given to ancient Israel, laws which were supplementary to the ten commandments. In the Confessions these are called 'sundry judicial laws'. We quote the 1689 *Baptist Confession of Faith* (following the *Westminster Confession*): 'To them also *[the Jews]* He gave sundry judicial laws, which expired together with the state of that people, not obliging any now by virtue of that institution, their general equity only being of moral use.'

What did the writers of the Confessions mean by *general equity*? The term means *general fairness*. (The word *equity* derives from the Latin *aequus* – fair.)

These sundry judicial laws exhibit many *principles* of justice and fairness which we are to apply to our lives today, but the way in which they were applied in the state of Israel in ancient times is no longer relevant. Reconstructionists protest that this cannot be so, because all God's laws reflect His holy character, and so their divinely revealed application cannot possibly change. They overlook, however, a whole cluster of factors, all of which completely overthrow their line of reasoning.

In the following chapter we look at these factors and show why reconstructionism must be rejected as a credible exposition of God's Word, and must be regarded as a fundamental departure from Truth, full of potential danger for the churches of Christ.

4. The Limited Scope of Sundry Laws

IN THIS CHAPTER we advance four reasons why the 'sundry laws' of the Israelites (and their punishments) are entirely unsuitable for the purposes of world government, as claimed by reconstructionists.

First, the sundry laws of Moses are unsuitable for post-Jewish world government because they were specifically given to regulate and to bless a small, *agricultural* and *religious* community, equipped with minimal governing and law-enforcing bureaucracy. Many of these laws were clearly designed exclusively for the community to which they were addressed, throughout the period that their special national covenant lasted. It is therefore unnatural and forced to elevate these regulations to the status of laws designed for all nations in every age of the world.

An obvious example of an exclusively Jewish law is that which forbids the charging of interest to people of the Jewish race *(Deuteronomy 23.19)*. Examples of very 'parochial' laws, relevant only to an ancient, agricultural nation, are those which require the land to lie fallow every seventh year, and permit people to eat their fill while in their neighbour's vineyard or field *(Exodus 23.10-11; Deuteronomy 23.24-25)*.

We have already referred to one exclusively Jewish law banning Ammonites and Moabites, but what about the stern prohibition of the sale of land *(Leviticus 25.23)*? Here was another law which applied uniquely to that 'church' state and covenant nation. *Their* land belonged entirely to God, and they were only tenants. Incidentally, this one law demolishes all the economic theories of reconstructionists, which rely very heavily on the pre-eminence of private ownership of property. (They say that the eighth commandment *implies* that the private ownership of property should be the supreme principle of all economic life. In this they overlook *Leviticus 25*, and *1 Chronicles 29.15*, where David prays according to his clear understanding of the law – 'For we are sojourners before Thee, and tenants, as all our fathers were' *[NASB]*.)

Another law which proves the exclusively Jewish nature of many of the sundry laws is the severe restriction on horses and chariots, coupled with the requirement to proceed to battle even when hopelessly outnumbered and out-equipped *(Deuteronomy 17.16 and 20.1-4).** This law is given on account of their special status as God's nation – 'For the Lord your God is he that goeth with you, to fight for you against your enemies, to save you.'

Even the hygiene law governing the disposal of human waste is expressed in terms of Jewish exclusivity: 'For the Lord thy God walketh in the midst of thy camp . . . therefore shall thy camp be holy: that he see no unclean thing in thee, and turn away from thee' *(Deuteronomy 23.14)*. In citing a few examples we have not touched upon non-ceremonial religious obligations, such as the laws requiring the harvest first-fruits and first-born sons to be offered to the Lord *(Exodus 22.29-30)*, which were clearly laws suited only to a worshipping people. There are many proofs of the fact that the sundry judicial laws were framed for *that particular* covenant nation, and for no other people.

Secondly, the sundry laws of ancient Israel included a purpose which was unique to that community, namely, the maintenance of the greatest possible degree of purity in the camp of a very special people. They were a *chosen* people, privileged by God to be a holy

---

**Deuteronomy 17.16* is understood as a restriction on the military use of horses (which includes horse-drawn equipment) in the light of *Deuteronomy 20.1*, God's command to Joshua (see *Joshua 11.6, 9*) and David's apparent obedience to this restriction (see *2 Samuel 8.4* and *1 Chronicles 18.4*).

community to represent His name before the world. They were appointed to show forth His glories, to receive His Word, and ultimately to receive the Messiah. They were not like any other nation or people. To preserve a standard of godliness not practicable or feasible among nations generally, the sundry laws and their punishments were appended to the basic code of moral law.

Reconstructionists miss the obvious point when they fail to note that *only* Israel received this detailed form of law. As the psalmist exclaimed – 'He sheweth his word unto Jacob, his statutes and his judgments unto Israel. He hath not dealt so with any *[other]* nation: and as for his judgments, they have not known them' *(Psalm 147.19-20).* There is no *geographical* nation-state in the world today chosen by God, and subject to especially rigorous laws and punishments in order to maintain the greatest possible purity. Although all people are under God's law, and all will one day be judged by it, their judgement lies in the future. (Incidentally, it staggers the imagination to think how many millions of people would perish by the death sentence if the laws of Israel were to be applied as criminal law throughout the world. The great commission would be rendered almost irrelevant!)

The company of redeemed people is the chosen nation of God today. They must apply in their lives the *principles* enshrined in the sundry laws, but certainly not the punishments, because the New Testament prescribes different punishments. As we have noted, the Corinthian sinner was not excluded from the congregation by stoning, but by expulsion.

The Scripture does not teach that the punishments attached to the sundry laws were God's sole and permanently appointed punishments for the crimes mentioned. They were simply the punishments which God chose for that community at that time. We must not forget that *full* justice is meted out to sinners on the day of judgement, and *any* punishments prescribed on earth can never fully fit the crime. Nowhere in the New Testament is there the slightest hint of an ancient Israelite punishment being applied in the church. On the other hand, various passages prescribe *quite different* disciplinary measures to offenders in the church.* The punishments of the Mosaic code were quite clearly designed to keep *that particular community* as pure as possible in view of its special calling.

Thirdly, the sundry laws are not suitable as the basis of general law internationally because many were framed primarily to teach a principle. The particular act to be performed was often prescribed chiefly because it conveyed a religious lesson to the people.

---

*Matthew 18.15-17; Romans 16.17; 1 Corinthians 5; 2 Thessalonians 3.6, 14; Titus 3.10-11; 2 John 10.

The obvious and oft-quoted example is the 'sundry law' – 'Thou shalt not muzzle the ox when he treadeth out the corn' *(Deuteronomy 25.4)*. Paul shows the real purpose of this law when he applies it to the support of preachers in *1 Corinthians 9.9-10*: 'Doth God take care for oxen? Or saith he it altogether for our sakes? For our sakes, no doubt, this is written.' The ancient Israelites kept that particular law, and, as they did so, they learned a vital principle – that the labourer is worthy of his hire. God taught them the principle at its very lowest level of application so that they would say to themselves, 'If we must have regard for the oxen, *how much more* must we take care to provide for our servants, and *how much more still* those who minister spiritual things.'

Other examples of sundry laws which taught an underlying principle are to be seen in the command to place a balustrade around the flat roof of a house; the command not to sow different varieties of seed in a field; the command not to cross-breed cattle; and the command not to make garments of mixed materials *(Leviticus 19* and *Deuteronomy 22)*. Taken at a literal level, these commands do not show the mind of God (or His character) with regard to roof design, clothing, etc. In the case of the 'mixing' laws the people were taught the importance of separation, and that things of entirely different moral or spiritual character should not be mingled together. The lessons were, for example

– do not try to serve God *and* mammon, and do not mix the worship of Jehovah with idolatry.

We are taught by Paul that everything which happened to the Israelites – 'happened unto them for ensamples: and they are written for our admonition, upon whom the ends of the world are come' *(1 Corinthians 10.11)*. Ultimately, God designed all the sundry and ceremonial laws, not only to teach the Israelites, but also to teach *believers* in the Gospel age. Many of these laws had an immediate, practical purpose in regulating conduct. But all taught abiding principles, often religious principles, and it is these principles which we as the Lord's people today desire to understand. We are not to attempt to continue the outward forms of *all* those laws, but to recognise their teaching and their message.

Fourthly, the sundry laws of Israel are not suitable for the practical regulation of secular nations because they included in their scope a message or sermon from God. They were partly intended to be a standard of righteousness unattainable by sinful human beings, in order to discourage and dismay their pride and self-confidence. Let us not forget that these sundry laws were given as part of a package which, if perfectly observed by the people as a whole, would have secured the rewards of righteousness for their nation – but this proved utterly impossible. The law – including the ceremonial and the sundry laws – was designed to drive the Jews to the message of grace which was strapped alongside it. Many sundry laws, taken individually, were most reasonable and observable, but taken as a whole they demanded a standard of behaviour far above the capability of unregenerate people.

Paul had in mind the entire law, including the ceremonial and sundry laws, when he said – 'Wherefore the law was our schoolmaster to bring us unto Christ . . . But after that faith is come, we are no longer under a schoolmaster' *(Galatians 3.24-25)*. Reconstructionists fail to grasp that the ancient law could never be a practical ideal for all nations, but only a daunting reminder of the unattainable heights of 'justification by works'.

This is clear from *Leviticus 18.4-5*, which is given in the context of the sundry laws: 'Ye shall do my judgments, and keep mine ordinances . . . which if a man do, he shall live in them' *[ie: a man will live if he does them]*. This is quoted by Paul in *Romans 10.5* – 'The man which doeth those things shall live by them.'

It is important to note that God Himself, exercising the prerogative of mercy, did not enforce either immediately or rigorously the prescribed punishments of the ancient law. Special and terrible punishments which would be directly administered by God were announced in *Leviticus 26.14-41* and *Deuteronomy 28.15-68*. God, however, made allowances for the sinfulness of the people throughout their history, and constantly delayed and deferred the punishment of destruction which had been announced at Sinai for their dis-obedience.

In *Ezekiel 20.11* and *13-14* the prophet makes this very same point: 'I gave them my statutes, and shewed them my judgments, which if a man do, he shall even live in them . . . But the house of Israel rebelled against me in the wilderness . . . and they despised my judg-ments . . . then I said, I would pour out my fury upon them in the wilderness, to consume them. But I wrought *[acted]* for my name's sake, that it should not be polluted before the heathen . . . *[cf verses 21-22]* Then I said, I would pour out my fury upon them, to accomplish my anger against them in the wilderness. Nevertheless I withdrew mine hand, and wrought for my name's sake . . .'

Here we see reflected again the mercy of God in post-poning judgement to the final day, rather than instantly imposing the penalties of which they had been warned. In *Nehemiah 9.21-31* the forbearance of God over many years is again recorded. Why did the Lord so often withhold due punishment, and show mercy? Because His conduct towards them in the 'Law Age' was a message, teaching them that mercy and pardon flow freely from the heart of Almighty God, and that salvation is by grace alone and not by works. Recon-structionist writers entirely fail to see the message element in the laws of the Jews, and in the oft-suspended divine punishment. The civil law-code of

Israel, therefore, was partly a *sermon* or message about the impossibility of justification by works, rather than a practical civil code for all the nations of the world.

Reference has already been made to the doctrinal position of the Westminster and Baptist Confessions. What better than to conclude this chapter with some of their proof texts, confirming the passing of the literal provisions of the sundry laws of the national covenant established through Moses.

The passing of this national law-system at the coming of Christ is anticipated in *Genesis 49.10* where God gave a prophetic word to Jacob: 'The sceptre shall not depart from Judah, nor a lawgiver from between his feet, until Shiloh come; and unto him shall the gathering of the people be.' The passing of the national law-system is confirmed by Paul in *Ephesians 2.15*, when he speaks of its removal at the inauguration of the multinational church of Christ: 'Having abolished in his flesh the enmity, even the law of commandments contained in ordinances; for to make in himself of twain one new man, so making peace.' What ordinances did Paul have in mind? Which laws were abolished? Without doubt he refers to both the ceremonial laws and the so-called sundry laws of *Exodus 21-23* and elsewhere.

The Greek word in *Ephesians 2.15,* which is translated *abolished,* is a very powerful word. It literally means: *having brought down to inactivity,* or *having made utterly useless, idle or void.* Paul would never have said this about the moral law expressed in the ten commandments. Indeed he says the opposite when he has in mind only the moral aspects of the law. In *Romans 3.31* he declares – 'Do we then make void *[the same Greek verb as above]* the law through faith? God forbid.' However, when he has in mind the Jewish law-code in its *entirety*, including ceremonial and sundry laws, he unhesitatingly speaks of it being reduced to inactivity, or being made void.

The Word of God is therefore clear in its teaching that the sundry laws, along with the ceremonial laws, are now 'abolished' or void – *in the form that they were given* to the Jews of old. The principles which underlie them live on for the Lord's people. But as far as *literal* obedience is concerned, they are rendered inactive, and no longer in force for the Lord's people. They are certainly not intended to serve as the civil and criminal code for the secular world.

5. The Church Not to Run the World

RECONSTRUCTIONIST writers all scorn the attitude of traditional evangelicals who see the church as being distinct and separate from the world, and who seek no authority over the affairs of the world. These writers should take careful note of the words of Paul in *1 Corinthians 5.12-13*: 'For what have I to do to judge them also that are without? do not ye judge them that are within? But them that are without God judgeth.' God is especially concerned with His people. He will not give His kingdom to the world nor will He give the world to His kingdom. The kingdom of God is the church, small as it may sometimes appear, not the world. The Lord said – 'Fear not, *little flock*; for it is your Father's good pleasure to give you the kingdom' *(Luke 12.32)*.

The world is, of course, under the moral law and the judgement of God, but it is not the work of God's people to administer the law. God has ordained civil magistrates, and put it into the hearts of human beings to desire and to accept their rule. *Romans 13.1-7* is Paul's great statement on the state's responsibility to administer justice, and also on the Christian's responsibility to obey, and also to pay the taxes demanded. In *1 Peter 2.13-14* we are similarly exhorted to obey the laws of the state (without chafing, or desiring to replace them with the laws of Moses): 'Submit yourselves to every ordinance of man for the Lord's sake: whether it be to the king, as supreme; or unto governors, as unto them that are sent by him for the punishment of evildoers, and for the praise of them that do well.'

It is interesting to note that the Mosaic law (held up by reconstructionists as the perfect model for world government) had no taxation, only freewill offerings. Taxes for general purposes came in with Solomon's twelve taxation districts, his value added tax on trading caravans, and the imposition of compulsory unpaid labour for the crown. The Saviour (our perfect example and pattern) paid the tax required by the secular state (in *Matthew 17.24-27*), and the apostle Paul commanded the payment of taxes. Neither attempted to do what Dr Bahnsen insists is our Christian duty – to persuade the secular power to adopt and enforce the Mosaic code of criminal and civil law. The New

Testament churches mounted no political campaigns for social or political dominion. Paul – whose example is normative for us to imitate – commanded obedience to the secular state even though he lived and moved in morally decadent and largely pagan territories.

The Lord Jesus Christ made it abundantly clear in His great prayer of *John 17* that we are not of this world. He taught His disciples in *John 15.18-21* that the world would hate and persecute them. Through the *Book of Revelation* we are shown the constant antagonism of this godless world to the true church of the Saviour. Where is the secular dominion of which the reconstructionists speak?

Reconstructionism is proving to be powerfully captivating to numbers of Christians, and also highly damaging to their New Testament perspectives. Where it takes root it seems to 'upstage' evangelism and preoccupy its devotees with endless discussion of social, economic, educational and political theories. In many cases it leads in a subtle way to rampant worldliness. (After all, if Christians are commissioned to take dominion over the arts, and so on, they had better start by participating in them and enjoying them.)

Where Christians have previously attempted to construct even a very limited Christian society their efforts have been sadly frustrated. Whether the sought-after society was Genevan, American-Puritan, Kuyperian or simply the latter-day efforts of the American 'Moral

Majority', the fruit has always either been negligible or short-lived. None of these campaigns envisaged anything more than a limited, regional Christian community, but even so, success eluded them. It is now said that all the enthusiasm, power and dollars of the 'Moral Majority' failed to secure one single significant piece of moral legislation in the USA.

None of this, however, dampens the ambition or optimism of reconstructionists. Their programme is infinitely more bold and far-reaching than anything considered before, and their confidence is seemingly boundless.

Reconstructionism has already won admirers in the UK, which is perhaps not surprising with so much 'reformed romanticism' about. Friends who experience little immediate blessing, but who rest *entirely* on a hoped-for revival, seem to be especially vulnerable to a movement which promises the earth, as well as heavenly blessings in the future. (To some, social dominion has become almost the due payment of a debt; fair compensation for enduring a long day of small things.) Where practical, zealous evangelism has been abandoned, leading to loss of blessing, and frustration, triumphalistic heresies such as reconstructionism offer a new significance and standing to enfeebled Christians. The trouble is that the goal it holds out is both fleshly *and* delusory. And the cost of attempting this foolish goal is a lifetime's 'labouring for the wind'. May the Lord's servants remain wholly dedicated to the work of the Gospel, and avoid being drawn into an unbiblical and unhealthy interest in the social reconstruction of a doomed world.

The stark fact remains that dominion of the world, massive aim as it is, is nowhere on the agenda of the New Testament for the servants of Christ. The apostle Paul's words must surely stand as the final sentence on the matter: 'No man that warreth entangleth himself with the affairs of this life; that he may please him who hath chosen him to be a soldier' *(2 Timothy 2.4).*

Appendix 1
Matthew 5.17-18

Think not that I am come to destroy the law, or the prophets: I am not come to destroy [abolish], but to fulfil. For verily I say unto you, Till heaven and earth pass, one jot or one tittle shall in no wise pass from the law, till all be fulfilled (Matthew 5.17-18).

WHEN THE LORD referred to 'the law, or the prophets' in *Matthew 5.17* He used the customary designation for the Pentateuch (the books of Moses) plus the rest of the Old Testament. Every part is inspired Scripture and will be fulfilled.

The moral law and all the principles of righteousness taught by Moses and the prophets were *fulfilled* with the coming of Christ because His saving power brought about full obedience to God's standards, and because His teaching made them fully clear.

The law involved much more than acts of external

obedience (as the Pharisees imagined). It involved *inner* obedience also – holiness of thoughts, motives and desires. It involved avoidance of 'sins of the heart' (unbelief, pride, greed, etc), an area of holiness totally disregarded by the Pharisees. By contrast Christ's disciples were taught (and still are) to accept a *complete* agenda of holiness, and also given the power and inclination to pursue it.

Of course, the Lord Jesus fulfilled the law and the prophets in other ways also. He *kept* the moral law perfectly for and on behalf of His redeemed people. He also fulfilled all the prophecies of the Old Testament, both those represented in the types and shadows of the ceremonial law, and the Messianic promises given through the prophets.

Also, by His power, He has already fulfilled many other prophecies in the Old Testament – prophecies of a glorious, soul-winning church in the last age of the world. And ultimately, He will bring in the fulfilment of the 'last days' predictions.

Christ's fulfilment of the law and the prophets is a ministry vastly greater and grander than the literal reimposition of the sundry judicial laws of ancient Israel!

Appendix 2
Dominion Theology, Blessing or Curse?

AFTER THE PRECEDING assessment of reconstructionism was written, the present author reviewed *Dominion Theology, Blessing or Curse?* by H. Wayne House and Thomas Ice, published in the USA by Multnomah Press. (H. Wayne House then served as a lecturer at Dallas Theological Seminary, and Thomas Ice as a pastor in Texas.) The review is reproduced here because *Dominion Theology* is such a well-informed assessment of the reconstructionist movement.

Wayne House and Thomas Ice attack reconstructionism chiefly at its postmillennial foundations (the authors are premillennialists), but many other arguments are also used, and an abundance of interesting supplementary information is provided.

Thomas Ice explains that for fourteen years he was a keen reconstructionist, despite maintaining his premillennial convictions. It was his inability to see scriptural justification for the reconstructionist scenario of Christian global conquest that finally led him to abandon the movement. As a reconstructionist, Pastor Ice testifies to having experienced the intellectual exhilaration of possessing all the answers to the problems of society. But he also felt the frustration of never seeing any genuine progress toward the longed-for social dominion.

These two authors give an illuminating overall picture of the American reconstructionist scene, providing details of all the leaders and many key writers. We learn that the movement's prominent author Dr Greg Bahnsen was dismissed from Reformed Seminary, Jackson, Mississippi, because of his reconstructionist 'heresy'.

We are told how the late Francis Schaeffer (as well as his son Franky) was deeply influenced by the movement in his later years. We learn also that twenty million charismatics around the world have adopted reconstructionism – according to the movement's patriarch, Dr Rousas Rushdoony. The authors identify these broadly as being the 'positive confession' wing, or the 'name-it-and-claim-it', or 'use-your-authority-in-

Christ' type of charismatics. We would add the 'pros-
perity gospel' teachers to the list. Reconstructionist
author Dr Gary North apparently shares the charismatic position that, 'God does not want His people to
be poor and sick.'

In this book the reconstructionist position is carefully
defined as teaching that only the ceremonial laws of the
Old Testament ended at the death of Christ. *All* others,
namely the moral law plus the sundry laws, must be
established as the law-basis of a Christian-dominated
world, which all Christians are duty-bound to bring
about.

One chapter in this book goes forward in imagination
to the year 40,255 AD and views an American republic
reformed according to the ideas of reconstructionists.
(Reconstructionists do give themselves an enormous
time-span to accomplish their goals.)

Allowing for differences of view among reconstructionists (which are considerable), a land is described
where only born-again Christians are allowed into government, all schools are run by churches, government
is decentralised, the death sentence is applied to
numerous offences, restitution is paramount in justice
('an eye for an eye'), 'voluntary' slavery is allowed, long
mortgages and other large debts are outlawed, and all
public services are privatised.

In this reconstructed USA, the old constitution has
been rewritten to remove religious liberty and

toleration – only evangelical Christianity being permitted. (The authors complain that if Dr Rousas
Rushdoony's ideas are adopted even dispensationalists
will be in fear of execution, as he is on record as regard-
ing their point of view as 'unbelief and heresy'.)

In a section challenging the boasts of reconstructionists to have Calvin and the Puritans on their side, this
book briefly yet effectively exposes the simplistic folly
of such claims.[*] A chapter entitled *Are Christians Under
the Mosaic Law?* deals emphatically with the reconstructionist claim that in *Matthew 5.17-20* the Lord
Jesus stated that He came to *confirm* the entire legal
demands of the Old Testament, thus confirming them
as the literal rule of life for His disciples and also for the
whole world. Recognising this claim as a vital foundation of reconstructionism, the authors demonstrate
most effectively the faulty exegesis of Bahnsen and others in turning *fulfil* into *confirm*. They advance solid
arguments in favour of the conventional interpretation
of the passage.

The authors deal equally well with the 'dominion
mandate' of *Genesis 1.28*, showing that the command of

---

[*]Among other reconstructionist claims which are ably
refuted, is the one advanced by Greg Bahnsen – that the
Westminster Confession supports their position. This is
based, as these authors show, on a far-fetched and novel
interpretation (or rather, bending) of the term 'general
equity'.

God gives mankind, as a whole, dominion over the animals and the earth, but that people are not given authority over other people. Conquest of anyone by anyone does not lie within the scope of this mandate. The idea that our Lord's great commission is merely a recapitulation of the dominion mandate of *Genesis* is most competently dismissed.

Reconstructionists must obviously take a view of the *Book of Revelation* which will allow scope for their scenario of Christian victory and dominion. The view of *Revelation* taken by evangelical amillennialists and premillennialists does not satisfy them at all, for the latter groups see in *Revelation* a picture of progressive apostasy, especially in the last days of the world, and great conflict between the world and the true church. Consequently, if biblical prophecy points to believers being *socially* persecuted in the last days, then reconstructionism must be dismissed as fallacy.

Not surprisingly, therefore, reconstructionists take a 'preterist' view of *Revelation*. According to this view, the *Book of Revelation* describes the situation in the time of John, its author, all the events having taken place during John's lifetime. (Some preterists regard the final chapters as predictive prophecy.) This view of *Revelation* claims that all the apostasy and persecution occurred at the very beginning of the Christian era, leaving the way clear to imagine a future in which there will be gradual world dominion for Christians.

Authors Wayne House and Thomas Ice focus much of their fire on the preterist approach to *Revelation*, and though they write from a premillennial point of view, most of their arguments would equally please amillennial readers. They trace the history of the preterist viewpoint back to a Jesuit priest named Alcasar, who devised this approach in order to escape from the teaching of the Reformers, who were identifying the Roman Church with the Babylon of *Revelation*. The preterist interpretation did not really gain ground among Protestants until German liberals took it up in the nineteenth century. They were naturally cynical about anything prophetic, and were further attracted to preterism because it helped them to dismiss the doctrine of the literal, personal return of the Lord Jesus Christ.

Much of the material in two chapters of this book *(The Olivet Discourse and Interpreting Prophecy)* appealed less to this reviewer, as it reflects the distinctive reasoning of dispensationalism. However, after these chapters the book proceeds to a survey of the dangers of reconstructionism, and so provides yet another wave of valuable comment.

There is interesting reference to the work of the great Abraham Kuyper (1837-1920), the Dutch pastor and theologian who founded the Free University of Amsterdam and who became Prime Minister of the Netherlands from 1901-1905. He is claimed by reconstructionists to be one of them, but, as these authors point out, Kuyper and his colleagues were only seeking to protect their church and families from the poison of humanism, not to dominate the world and bring it under the rule of the Mosaic civil code. Although Kuyper made a great impact on his generation, the social ethos he created in the Netherlands could not be sustained for long, and suffered startlingly rapid decline and reaction, providing further evidence of the untenability of such social adventures, however well intended.

This book demonstrates that reconstructionists, Calvinists though they may be, become Arminian in their social aspirations, because they greatly underestimate the depravity of human nature. (There is even a portion which shows how the founders – all students of Van Til – have betrayed their mentor through this movement.) The authors show that reconstructionists' concern for the preaching of the Gospel becomes secondary to their social and political ambitions and interests. They point out that just as postmillennialism once provided the climate for the rise of the 'social gospel', so it now nourishes another essentially social endeavour in reconstructionism.

Altogether, this is a most valuable (and lively) treatment of reconstructionism which will be appreciated by pastors and others who have a need to be informed about this movement. It runs to 460 pages, and includes extensive bibliographical notes on the books and magazines issued by the principal reconstructionist authors.

Appendix 3
Theonomy: A Reformed Critique

Theonomy: A Reformed Critique; editors: William S. Barker & W. Robert Godfrey, 1990, Zondervan Publishing House, Grand Rapids.

THIS WORK APPEARED nearly a year after the publication of the material in the present book. It is a 413-page critique of reconstructionism, of special interest to those pastors and thinkers who wish to evaluate the matter intensively. Significantly, all the contributors are from the reformed Presbyterian constituency within which the movement arose. The editors are professors of church history at Westminster Theological Seminary, USA, and all the other contributors are professors or lecturers at the Seminary.

'The focus of this collection of sixteen essays,' states the publisher, 'is the effect of theonomy on churches and Christian people.' The desire of the authors 'is to offer a constructive critique of the Christian reconstruction movement. As they see it, theonomy in various ways represents a distorted view of continuities and discontinuities between the Old Testament and our time.'

The editors explain the plan of the work in the following way:–

'Part I seeks to provide basic orientations to the matter of application of biblical law. Part II contrasts theonomy with other systematic approaches to biblical theology. Part III deals with New Testament teaching concerning the nature of the continuity of Old Testament law. Part IV addresses what we perceive as triumphalist dangers in theonomy. Part V is concerned with the historical question of theonomy's relation to the heritage of John Calvin and the Puritans. The conclusion seeks to end the volume with a constructive challenge to theonomy.'

The sixteen essays (chapters) are as follows:–

1. *May We Use the Term 'Theonomy' for Our Application of Biblical Law?* Professor Robert D. Knudsen.

2. *God's Law and Mosaic Punishments Today.* Dr Tremper Longman III.

3. *Theonomy in Relation to Dispensational and Covenant Theologies.* Professor Bruce K. Waltke.

4. *The One, the Many, and Theonomy.* Professor John M. Frame.

5. *Effects of Interpretive Frameworks on the Application of Old Testament Law.* Professor Vern S. Poythress.

6. *The New Testament Use of the Pentateuch: Implications for the Theonomic Movement.* Dr Dan G. McCartney.

7. *Is the Law Against the Promises? The Significance of Galatians 3.21 for Covenant Continuity.* Professor Moisés Silva.

8. *The Epistle to the Hebrews and the Mosaic Penal Sanctions.* Dr Dennis E. Johnson.

9. *Theonomy and Eschatology: Reflections on Postmillennialism.* Professor Richard B. Gaffin, Jr.

10. *Theonomy, Pluralism, and the Bible.* Professor William S. Barker.

11. *The Theonomic Attraction.* John R. Muether.

12. *Theonomy and the Poor: Some Reflections.* Dr Timothy J. Keller.

13. *Calvin and Theonomy.* Professor W. Robert Godfrey.

14. *An Assembly of Theonomists? The Teaching of the Westminster Divines on the Law of God.* Professor Sinclair B. Ferguson.

15. *New England Puritans and the State.* Professor Samuel T. Logan, Jr.

16. *A Challenge to Theonomy.* Professor D. Clair Davis.

Other Wakeman books by Dr Peter Masters

The Charismatic Phenomenon
Peter Masters & John C. Whitcomb
113 pages, paperback, ISBN 1 870855 01 9

Dr Masters, and Dr Whitcomb (co-author of the renowned work – *The Genesis Flood*), together trace the purpose of the sign-miracles and revelatory gifts of New Testament times, and their precise nature. Were they intended to be ongoing in the life of the Church? Numerous questions are here answered, such as, 'What exactly are the greater works of *John 14.12*?' and 'Are the signs following, referred to in *Mark 16*, for today?' This easy-to-read work has been helpful to many thousands having passed through six printings in an earlier edition, and three in this present edition (not to mention many translations into other languages).

The Healing Epidemic
Peter Masters
227 pages, paperback, ISBN 1 870855 00 0

The *Healing Epidemic*, now in its fourth major printing, was commended by the renowned American literary review *Bibliotheca Sacra* as – 'one of the best books on this subject today. It should be widely read by concerned Christian people of all theological persuasions.'

The author first traces the origins of the current upsurge of healing ministries. He then takes each of the eleven main arguments used by healers in support of their methods, and shows the mistaken nature of each one. He provides important facts about demonology, showing just what demons can and cannot do. He proves from Scripture that the *sign*-gifts have ceased, and tells how *James 5* should be implemented in our churches today. He also presents the biblical commands that the conscious mind should always be alert and rational for all worship and spiritual service. The book includes an assessment of miraculous healing by a leading British medical specialist, Prof Verna Wright of Leeds University Medical School.

Biblical Strategies for Witness
Peter Masters
154 pages, paperback, ISBN 1 870855 18 3

'Perhaps it is not realised,' writes Dr Masters, 'just how much detailed and practical guidance is stored in the Gospels and the *Book of Acts* for all who engage in personal witness and preaching. Are we aware, for example, that the Lord Jesus Christ employed distinctive strategies for different kinds of unbeliever, and that these may be studied and copied? In addition, the Lord regularly employed several "techniques" for opening the minds of all listeners.'

Two chapters of this book focus upon the nature of the work of the Spirit in the soul in regeneration and conversion, distinguishing between the two, and showing the genuine instrumentality of persuasive Gospel pleading.

Only One Baptism of the Holy Spirit
Peter Masters
109 pages, paperback, ISBN 1 870855 17 5

Young Christians these days are confronted by much confusion on the teaching of the Holy Spirit and how He baptises, fills and anoints God's people. Contradictory statements and clashing ideas flow from a new generation of anecdotal-style books, which tend not to offer a close look at biblical passages on the subject.

In this book Dr Masters takes readers through Bible verses to establish each point, and to answer each question posed.

When is the believer baptised with the Spirit, and what does it amount to? Is there a second baptism? How exactly does the Spirit witness with our spirit? How does assurance come? Is the believer to struggle against sin, or does the Lord fight the battle for him? Must we be emptied and broken to receive the blessing? What is the filling of the Spirit?

Clear and scriptural answers are given to all such questions, and there is an appendix about the controversy over the 'Ephesus twelve', and whether or not their experience proves the need for a baptism of the Spirit *after* conversion.

Should Christians Drink?
The Case for Total Abstinence
Peter Masters
112 pages, paperback, ISBN 1 870855 12 4

What are the biblical arguments which have convinced the overwhelming majority of Bible believers for more than 150 years that the Lord wants His people to abstain? What are the great differences between the wine production of Bible times and the industry of today? Here is much information in a highly important book for these days in which long-held standards are challenged on every hand.

The Necessity of Sunday Schools
In this Post-Christian Era
Peter Masters & Malcolm H. Watts
112 pages, paperback, ISBN 1 870855 13 2

A clarion call for the unique effectiveness of *evangelistic* Sunday Schools operated on a large scale. This book offers invincible proof that the Bible sanctions and commands child evangelism of the kind represented by vigorous Sunday School outreach. The authors contend that there is no need for Sunday School numbers to fall, or for Schools to close. Christians should take a 'total neighbourhood responsibility' for the rising generation. Here is real stimulation and encouragement for the opening or enlargement of Sunday Schools, along with counsel and help for workers.

Men of Destiny/Men of Purpose

Men of Destiny and *Men of Purpose* are two very popular volumes of Christian biography, presenting the lives and conversion experiences of 25 famous, unusual or even notorious people, including royals, Reformers, and 'fathers' of modern science.

Given to unconverted people, these books challenge the heart and open the way to further spiritual influence. For the preacher, youth leader or Sunday School teacher, they provide outstanding testimonies to illustrate and enrich messages for years to come.

Men of Destiny
Peter Masters
172 pages, paperback, illustrated, ISBN 1 870855 03 5

Tsar Alexander Pavlovich *(The tsar who defeated Napoleon)*
Lieut 'Birdie' Bowers *(Scott's 'bravest man' in the Antarctic)*
Sir James Simpson *(The discoverer of anaesthetic chloroform)*
Alves Reis *(The counterfeiter who nearly owned his country)*
Joshua Poole *(The story of 'Fiddler Joss', drunkard turned preacher)*
Viscount Alexander of Hillsborough *(A leader of the House of Lords)*

John Newton *(The transformed slave-trader)*
Jean Henri Dunant *(Founder of the International Red Cross)*
Martin Luther *(The ex-monk who led the Reformation)*
Bilney, Tyndale & Latimer *(Three heroic English martyrs)*
Alfred the Great *(The king who organised England)*
Lieut-General Sir William Dobbie *(World War II hero of Malta)*

Men of Purpose
Peter Masters
167 pages, paperback, illustrated, ISBN 1 870855 04 3

Michael Faraday *(Father of electrical science)*
Henry J. Heinz *(Founder of the food empire)*
Felix Mendelssohn *(A composer with a spiritual journey)*
Lord Radstock *(Whose missions brought conversions to Russia's aristocracy)*
James Clerk Maxwell *(Father of modern physics)*
Philip P. Bliss *(The hymnwriter who won countless souls)*
Fred Charrington *(The brewer who renounced a fortune)*
Lord Kelvin *(Britain's greatest scientific inventor)*
James Montgomery *(A poet who ran away from God)*
Sir John Ambrose Fleming *(Inventor of the radio valve)*
Daniel Defoe *(The founder of journalism and great novelist)*

The Baptist Confession of Faith of 1689
Updated with notes by Peter Masters
91 pages, paperback, ISBN 1 870855 02 7

C. H. Spurgeon declared of this great *Confession* – 'Here the youngest members of our church will have a body of Truth in small compass, and by means of the scriptural proofs, will be able to give a reason of the hope that is in them.'

This brilliant summary of doctrine (in the same family as

the *Westminster Confession*), with its invaluable proof texts, has been gently updated in punctuation, and archaic words replaced. Helpful explanations of difficult phrases have been added in italic brackets. A brief history of the *Confession*, with an index, is included.

[Compiled by the leading divines among British Baptists in the 17th century and adopted by two assemblies of Baptist churches in 1677 and 1689.]

These books are available from Christian bookshops, or from the publisher: The Wakeman Trust, 5 Templar Street, London SE5 9JB. Tel: 071-735 7989